THE TRUTH ABOUT
ETERNITY
AND THE SPIRIT WORLD

Bryan P. Mistele

Beyond Today Publishing
Second Printing

Beyond Today Publishing
21311 NE 84th St.
Redmond, WA 98053

To order additional copies of this book on-line or obtain additional information about the author go to:

www.bryanmistele.com

To send comments, questions or feedback to the author, e-mail:

bryan@mistele.com

Printed in the United States of America

ISBN 0-9766845-1-9

TABLE OF CONTENTS

INTRODUCTION

"Set your minds on things above, not on earthly things."
(Colossians 3:2)

The Bible instructs us as believers to set our minds on things above—heavenly things as opposed to earthly things. We are to meditate and concentrate our thoughts on what exists beyond our own world. This is to impact our perspective on life and on the way we live each day. Indeed, what truly makes Christians different from most people is our belief in a parallel world—a spirit world—that is not a dwelling place of mankind, but rather the dwelling place of angels, demons, Satan, and God Himself. If Christians are truly to hold to the hope of our salvation, we must believe that such a place exists and this belief must be an active part in our faith.

In teaching opportunities and discussions I have had with numerous people, I have found that very few Christians truly understand or have studied the actual nature of the spirit world. If asked, most Christians will certainly acknowledge that a "heaven" and a "hell" exist and that there are angels and demons—but most are surprised to learn that the spirit world consists of many more places than just heaven and hell and that there are many different types of beings within the spirit world beyond just angels and demons. Furthermore, many are confused about what our existence will be like in the afterlife. Will we have physical bodies? Will we be angels? Will we be able to recognize our friends or still be married to our spouses? What about eternal rewards—do the things we do on earth during our human existence really influence for eternity our standing in heaven?

Will some people (perhaps Mother Teresa or Billy Graham) have more power or possessions in heaven than others? Why?

Very few understand how the spirit world exists now or could describe what the Bible says about how it will radically change in the future. Most people assume that when a person dies, they immediately go to either heaven or hell for eternity—the Christians go to heaven to be with God and all the angels, and the non-Christians go to hell to be tormented by Satan and his demons for eternity. This statement is incomplete and isn't true for several reasons. First, there are many locations in the spirit world including paradise, heaven, hades, Tartarus, the abyss, and the lake of fire (otherwise known as hell). Depending upon the point in time a person dies and whether that person is a believer or not will determine which location a person will go to within the spirit world. Second, although heaven and hades exist today and people do go there upon death, these are only temporary places, which the Bible states will be destroyed at some point in the future. As such, people will not spend eternity in either the heaven or hell that they think of today. Third, God, Satan, the angels and the demons are not actually confined to, or contained within heaven or hell since at present they have the freedom to travel between these places as well as earth at will. Finally, Satan and the demons will not be doing any tormenting in hell for eternity. Rather, they themselves will be tormented along with those that consciously rejected God during their lifetimes.

We will explore each of these points as well as many others in more detail throughout this booklet. I have structured this booklet in a question and answer format to address the most common questions I have heard from people regarding the nature of the afterlife. My purpose in writing this article is simply to provide a general overview of the spirit world (both now and in the future) so that Christians can better "set [their] minds on things above" as the Bible instructs us to do.

WHY MUST WE DIE?

Perhaps the most fundamental question when studying the nature of the afterlife is the most basic: Why must we die at all? Why couldn't God have simply created mankind in such a way that we never die— we just enjoy creation and an eternal existence here on earth or perhaps in heaven with Him? Sounds nice, doesn't it? We wouldn't have to worry about sick or dying family members, heaven and hell, or doing (or not doing) things in this lifetime that may impact our lives in eternity.

The answer to this question lies in the story of Adam and Eve and their account in the Garden of Eden as recorded in the book of Genesis. "In the beginning" we are told, "God created the heavens and the earth" (Genesis 1:1) and pronounced them "very good" (Genesis 1:31). He then created Adam and Eve in a perfect setting— a setting free from sin where He could interact with mankind in a very personal and relational manner. In fact, God Himself walked among Adam and Eve in the garden, and we are told that Adam and Eve could hear the sound of His walking (Genesis 3:8). This clearly indicates that for Adam and Eve, God was not an abstract concept or silent deity. Rather, God had a somewhat human form (at the very least capable of walking) and interacted with His creation in a very real and tangible manner.

Of course, we all know the story of the fall—when Adam and Eve ate the apple and disobeyed God. However, what's interesting to note about this story is the consequence of this original sin. When God warned Adam and Eve not to eat from the tree he told them not to do so because they would "die". Satan actually took advantage of this statement and used it to challenge Eve when he was tempting her by saying "you will not surely die" (Genesis 3:4). The consequence of sin is physical death, we are told, but why?

The answer, believe it or not, is God's grace. When Adam and Eve sinned against God, they forfeited their ability to have a direct, personal relationship with a present God. God cannot be in the presence of sin, so when Adam and Eve sinned, God had to separate mankind from Himself. He physically banished Adam and Eve from the garden and never again allowed mankind to have direct interaction with Him (Genesis 3:22–24). Therefore, God had two alternatives—either allow mankind to live forever as sinners on earth eternally separated from Him without any means of restoration, or introduce death as a means to reunite Himself with mankind. Given these choices, God chose the latter, which is why He originally told Adam that death would be the consequence if he ate from the forbidden fruit. Satan, in his challenge to Eve, was implying that *immediate* death would not be the consequence of eating the apple. This is true—what God meant was that *eventual* death would be the consequence of sin.

Interesting

Death, then, is God's way of reuniting ourselves to Him. This is why Christ said when He was on earth "do not fear those who kill the body, but are unable to kill the soul; but rather fear Him who is able to destroy both the soul and the body in hell" (Matthew 10:28). We are not to fear physical death, because death rescues us from an endless existence apart from God and brings us eventually into His presence, where we can once again have a direct and personal relationship with Him as He originally intended.

Because of this, we should never say that a believer "has departed", but rather our perspective should be that "he has arrived". Death is never an accident because God is sovereign over all things—including the timing and the nature of our deaths. Whether we die from medical conditions, car accidents, or at the hands of criminals or unjust men, God uses these events to bring His people home. We should not forget that Christ Himself was killed early in His life by unjust men, yet Scripture tells us many times that this was "God's appointed hour" for Him. There is never a case when someone dies 'prematurely'—everyone dies precisely when God has ordained they will. Having said that, it's OK to feel apprehensive about facing death. We should not feel guilty about this because Christ Himself died with a mixture of both grief and joy (Matthew 26:38; John 17:5; Hebrews 12:2).

WHERE DO WE GO WHEN WE DIE?

When people die, they face two very different alternative destinations. The first alternative is to be in the direct presence of God and experience His love forever in a very real and wonderful place. The second alternative is to forever be apart from God in a place of unending regret and suffering—a place of real pain and torment where guilt and abandonment will be with you forever.

Although you may think these descriptions of heaven and hell are too cliché, left over from some medieval scare tactic to produce converts to the Church, or even perpetuated by well-intentioned parents wishing to keep their children in line, these descriptions are clearly taught and presented in the Bible. We will look at heaven and hell in more detail throughout this article, but the most convincing proof that these very real alternatives exist is the teaching of Christ Himself as presented in Luke 16:19–31. In this passage, Christ tells of a rich man and a beggar named Lazarus. When they died, Lazarus was taken by angels and carried to heaven, while the rich man was taken to hell where he was in torment. So much torment, in fact, that the rich man begged for pity and requested that Lazarus dip the tip of his finger in water to cool his tongue due to the agony from the fire he was experiencing. The important point to note about this story is that Christ did not present it as a parable—he presented it as a matter-of-fact account of these two people's lives. He wasn't necessarily trying to tell a story that had a moral point at the end. Rather, he was describing a very important aspect of the afterlife to the people and scholars who were listening to Him.

The key point is this—there is no middle ground between these two alternative destinations and no way to move between them once you die. Once life ends, a person will be taken to one of these two destinations forever. What then determines which destination you will end up at? Christ said "I am the way and the truth and the life. No one comes to the Father except through me" (John 14:6). With this, Jesus was making a very narrow and exclusive statement—that no one can be saved except through Him. He was proclaiming that He is the one and only way to salvation. This is what sets Christianity apart from all other world's religions. Namely, that salvation is based on *faith in what Jesus did* and not on faith in *what we can do*. When Christ came and died on the cross, He became the ultimate sacrifice. Now a person can be saved simply by accepting the pardon for sin that Christ provided through His death. All people on the earth have already been pardoned—the issue is whether or not a person will accept Christ's pardon for their sins.

The obvious question, then, is: What must a person do to be saved? Over 200 times in the Bible, faith, or belief, is stated as the single condition for salvation. The Bible is clear—a person must simply accept the free gift of Christ's sacrifice on the Cross. Salvation is a gift, and all one needs to do is reach out and accept it. The Bible says: "For the wages of sin is death, but the free gift of God is eternal life in Christ Jesus our Lord." (Romans 6:23). Everyone has sinned. Being 'good' is not enough in God's eyes. The Bible says: "all have sinned and fall short of the glory of God". (Romans 3:23). How can one come to know God? The Bible says:

"For God so loved the world, that He gave His one and only son, that whoever believes in Him shall not perish but have eternal life. For God did not send His Son into the world to condemn the world, but to save the world through Him. Whoever believes in Him is not condemned, but whoever does not believe stands condemned already because he has not believed in the name of God's one and only Son." (John 3:16–18)

"If you confess with your mouth, 'Jesus is Lord,' and believe in your heart that God raised Him from the dead, you will be saved. For it is with your heart that you believe and are justified, and it is with your mouth that you confess and are saved." (Romans 10:9–10)

Everyone who acknowledges that he or she is a sinner, believes in Jesus Christ and His sacrifice on the cross, and puts his or her trust in Him will be saved. It's that simple. By then seeking to establish a relationship with Him through prayer, Bible study and fellowship in a local Church, one can grow in his or her relationship with Christ and further develop as a Christian.

In his book *One Minute After You Die*, author Erwin W. Lutzer said, "Unbelief is like people enjoying themselves at a party in a tall apartment building not knowing that there is a fire consuming the lower floors." This is sad, but true. To reject God or to live in unbelief is to ignore the reality of our existence and the nature of the afterlife revealed by God to us.

WHAT ABOUT PEOPLE WHO HAVEN'T HEARD OF CHRIST?

If everyone faces one of two possible destinations upon their death and their destination is based solely on whether or not they have accepted Christ during their lifetime, then what about those who haven't heard of Christ? What about people who live in Africa and haven't had the opportunity to hear the gospel? What about babies or children who died while they were young? What about people who grew up in Buddhist or Muslim households and accepted the faith of their parents? Isn't it grossly unfair for God to hold them to account in eternity for something they were never really exposed to on earth or were too young to understand?

These are good questions, and the Bible doesn't answer them directly. However, we can make several assumptions based on a couple of biblical truths. The first of these is that *all* have sinned (Romans 3:10; 3:23). There is no one on the earth who is 'innocent' or sinless independent of God's grace. This includes infants and children. Romans 5:12 states plainly "sin entered the world through one man, and death through sin, and in this way death came to all men because all sinned." However, the second basic truth is that God is loving, holy, and just. It's certainly not in His character to unfairly judge people who haven't heard of the Gospel or little ones who were too young to understand. In fact, several times Jesus specifically called out children as being near to His heart and even instructed his disciples to become like children in their faith if they wished to be great in the kingdom of heaven (Matthew 18:1–6, 10–14, 19:14). Clearly, God admires the sense of openness, trust, and dependency that children have. Therefore, it's reasonable to assume that God will only hold children accountable for what they were able to comprehend, should they die at a young age. God certainly will not hold children responsible for doing what they could not do.

Throughout most of history, the Church has held the doctrine of an 'age of accountability'—the concept being that before a certain age, God does not hold children accountable for consciously accepting or rejecting Christ. It's only when they are mature enough to comprehend the concepts of salvation, afterlife, and acceptance of Christ that they then become accountable for their actions. James 4:17 states "therefore, to one who knows the right thing to do, and does not do it, to him it is sin." The point being that someone must have enough of a mental capacity to understand right and wrong before they are held accountable for their actions. What is this age of accountability? It's likely different for every child based on their education, mental capacity, and maturity. The point is that God knows each person's heart and will judge each one accordingly. This would naturally apply to the mentally handicapped as well as children. The concept of the age of accountability, although not explicitly taught in Scripture, is mirrored in our judicial system, where different legal standards exist for minors than for adults.

There is also some biblical evidence for the salvation of children. When King David's infant son was struck with illness, David prayed, fasted and grieved deeply for the child, hoping that God would let the child live. However, when the child died, the Bible records that David got up, changed his clothes, washed, went to the Temple, and worshiped God. He then went to his house to eat. When questioned about this, David replied, "now that he is dead, why should I fast? Can I bring him back again? I will go to him, but he will not return to me" (2 Samuel 12:23). David clearly believed that he would eventually see his child again in heaven ("I will go to him") and worshiped God upon his death. We should take comfort in this fact as David did.

What about adults who haven't heard of the word? How will they be judged? Again, the Bible doesn't specifically answer these questions, but we can rest in the certainty that God is just and that he will judge each person individually and fairly. Similar to children, it would be grossly unfair to hold people accountable for faith in Christ who have never heard of Him. Nobody will go to hell for eternity due to a lack of knowledge or a low IQ. Rather, people will go to hell for rejecting the pardon that Jesus provided for their sins. Heaven is not an exclusive club for those with luck enough to have heard about how to get a ticket in. Rather, hell is a club for those who have consciously rejected God and decided to live their lives independent from Him. C.S. Lewis once wrote "There are only two kinds of people in the end: those who say to God, 'Thy will be done,' and those to whom God says, '*Thy* will be done.'" People will not end up in hell by accident, but rather by their own choice to reject God and His plan for salvation.

Having said that, The Bible clearly teaches that mankind has no excuse. Romans 1:20 states "For since the creation of the world God's invisible qualities—his eternal power and divine nature—have been clearly seen, being understood from what has been made, so that men are without excuse." Although people may never have heard of the first century person named Jesus Christ, this verse clearly teaches that God's qualities have been revealed in nature so that the rejection of God makes a man without excuse before God. Romans 2:14–16 goes on to say:

> "When Gentiles, who do not have the law, do by nature things required by the law, they are a law for themselves, even though they do not have the law, since they show that the requirements of the law are written on their hearts, their consciences also bearing witness, and their thoughts now accusing, now even defending them. This will take place on the day when God will judge men's secrets, through Jesus Christ, as my gospel declares."

The point here is that mankind has been given an innate sense of morality independent of "the law" (a reference to Scripture) and independent of Jesus Christ. Therefore, for those who have never heard the Gospel of Jesus, they will be held accountable for what they did know and have experienced. They will be accountable for the realization that God has revealed Himself through nature and for what their conscience has revealed to them. At the end of the Bible, the book of Revelation describes God's judgment of unbelievers (Revelation 20:11–15). It states, "each person was judged according to what he had done". Although no one is saved by personal works or deeds, these passages clearly show a different level of accountability (or 'bar') for people, depending on their personal knowledge of the Gospel. Salvation is a gift of God and is not based on what we do, but God will choose to extend this gift to those unfamiliar with the Gospel when He judges them based upon what they did know and what they did do with that knowledge. This is consistent with His character. If God is truly a just judge, then we would expect that everyone would receive a judgment precisely for what they deserved.

WHAT IS THE SPIRIT-WORLD LIKE?

Although most people think that the spirit world consists of just heaven and hell, the Bible actually describes at least seven distinct locations within the spirit world: paradise, heaven, hades, Tartarus, the Abyss, the 'new heaven and new earth' and the lake of fire (otherwise known as hell). The first five of these locations exist now, while the latter two will be created after the Millennium (a 1,000 year period of time which will occur after Christ has returned to the earth). Each of these locations within the spirit-world has its own distinct purpose and usefulness in God's plan. The diagram below illustrates these places:

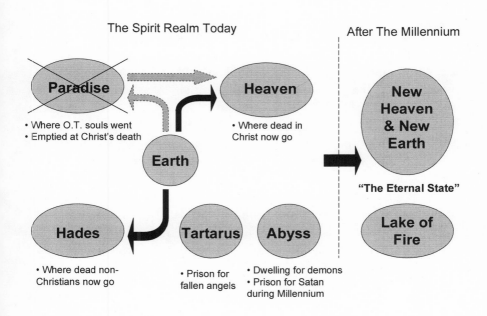

Paradise

It is believed that paradise was the place where the souls of Old Testament believers went upon their death. It is different than the heaven we think of today or where the souls of believers now go upon death. This was true until the time of Christ's resurrection. When Christ rose from the dead, it is believed that He emptied paradise and took the souls that were there to heaven with Him (Ephesians 4:8–10; Psalm 68:18). It's important to point out that there is some debate among Christian scholars regarding the existence of paradise due to limited scriptural evidence to support it, so no one should be dogmatic about its existence (or more accurately, its former existence). Proponents point to the different terminology used in the Old Testament and in some places in the New Testament that seem to differentiate it from heaven. For instance, when Christ Himself was on the cross, His words to the penitent thief hanging beside Him were, "today you will be with me in paradise" (Luke 23:43). This is similar terminology to what is used throughout the Old Testament, but yet different than what is used elsewhere in the New Testament following Christ's resurrection.

The reason proponents point to the necessary existence of paradise is because the Bible is clear that God is holy and cannot be in the presence of sin. In the Old Testament, people who lived under the Law prior to Christ's death had not had their sins washed away by the blood of Christ. The sacrificial system of sheep and other animals was symbolic of the sacrifice Christ would make. It was only upon the death of Christ—a sinless man and God's only son—that believers could then be allowed into the direct presence of God. As a result, paradise was necessary to separate Old Testament believers who were under the sacrificial law from God until the death and resurrection of Christ. It is for similar reasons that the veil of Holy of Holies in the Jewish Temple was torn in two by God upon Christ's death (Matthew 27:51). Namely, Christ's death facilitated a new relationship between God and man—one which enabled believers, for the first time since the fall of man in the Garden of Eden, to have a direct relationship and presence with God (Hebrews 10:19–20; Ephesians 2:14–18).

Regardless of your point of view, paradise is now empty and all Old Testament believers are now with God in heaven, which is also where believers now go upon their death.

Heaven

When Christians die today, their spirits are immediately taken to heaven, but this place is only a temporary location—it is not permanent. After the Millennium, the Bible says that God will destroy heaven and the earth and a "new heaven" and a "new earth" will be created. It is here that believers will spend eternity (2 Corinthians 12:2–4; Mark 16:19; Romans 8:34; Philippians 1:23).

So what is the heaven that exists now like? If we were to die today, where would we go? What is existence like for our departed friends or relatives who were believers? The Bible actually provides little physical detail about the current-day heaven, but what we do know is the following:

- Heaven is God's dwelling place—it is His home, center of operations, and throne room (Psalm 33:13–14; Isaiah 66:1; Matthew 6:9, 7:21,10:32–33; Revelation 7:9). However, God is not contained or confined there. God is not limited spatially to heaven since He is omnipresent—meaning that He is everywhere. 1 Kings 8:27 says "Behold heaven and the highest heaven cannot contain Thee" and Psalm 139:8 states "If I ascend to heaven, Thou are there; if I make my bed in Sheol, behold, Thou are there". God is everywhere, but clearly heaven is His primary place of residence or presence.

- God, the angels, and other beings in the spirit world can view the events that are taking place on earth (1 Corinthians 4:9; 1 Timothy 5:21). The Bible says that "from heaven the Lord looks down and sees all mankind; from His dwelling place He watches all who live on earth" (Psalm 33:13–14). Think about the implications of this—God and presumably others actually see us live our lives each day. Did you see the movie *The Truman Show* in which Jim Carey played a character whose life was constantly televised to millions of viewers? Perhaps life on earth is not too different. Really understanding this truth should cause us to rethink how we live our lives each day.

- Heaven has physical characteristics—it is more than just a mystical dreamland or meta-physical state. Christ stated that "In my Father's house are many rooms....I am going there to prepare a place for you" (John 14:2–3). Hebrews 11:16 states that God "has prepared a city" for believers. Clearly, heaven has physical residences and features similar to what we as humans would be familiar with. This should not be a surprise since the Bible tells us that we are created in God's image (Genesis 1:27). In the "new heaven" described below, actual measurable dimensions are given as well as physical descriptions of gates, foundation stones, and features such as rivers. Although it's difficult to compare the current heaven and the "new heaven", it's natural to conclude that the heaven that exists today has similar physical properties as opposed to being some sort of abstract collection of spirit beings. This conclusion is also supported by the Apostle John's account of when he was actually taken to heaven. This account is recorded in Revelation 4, and is the only eyewitness account the Bible contains of heaven. In his account, John described the throne room of God, including the colors that he saw and what he perceived as a sea. Therefore, although heaven doesn't have physical boundaries of time and space and isn't somewhere that physically could be found within the universe, it's logical to conclude that heaven does have some degree of physical properties not unlike what we know of today.

- People will be recognizable and will be able to recognize others. This will allow people to be united with family members who are there (Genesis 15:15, 49:33). We will discuss this more below in the section on eternal bodies, but our spirits in heaven will have identities that are directly linked to the personal identities we had on earth.

Hades

Hades is a place that holds the souls of unbelievers between their death and their ultimate demise—being cast into the lake of fire (otherwise known as hell). When unbelievers die, they are immediately taken to hades, which, like the current day heaven, is only a temporary location that will be destroyed by God after the Millennium and will be replaced with another place that will last for eternity. Hades is sometimes referred to as 'sheol', which is the Hebrew (Old Testament) word for the realm of the dead as opposed to 'hades', which is the Greek (New Testament) word. Hades is sometimes also called the 'place of torments.'

What is hades like? Unfortunately, much like the current day heaven, the Bible doesn't provide many physical details of hades. What we do know is:

- Hades was created as a place to accommodate Satan and the fallen angels that rebelled against God before the earth was created (Matthew 25:41). People that reject Christ will join Satan here upon their death.

- Much like God and heaven, Satan is not confined to hades—it is his dwelling place or center of operations, but it is only a common misconception that Satan and his demons are imprisoned there at present. Although Satan did rebel from God and is considered 'a fallen angel', Satan still has access to God in heaven and is free to roam the earth. Evidence of his ability to converse with God is found in Job: "One day the angels came to present themselves before the Lord and Satan also came with them" (Job 1:6). Evidence of his liberty to visit earth includes his appearance to Eve in the Garden of Eden (Genesis 3:1–5) and his appearance to Jesus in the wilderness (Matthew 4:1–11). Clearly, Satan has the ability to move between heaven, hades, and the earth as he desires. It will not be until the time of Armageddon, at the end of the current age, when Satan will be incarcerated and will no longer be free to roam the earth or do his own will.

- Hades is a place of real torment—the image most people likely have in their minds of it isn't too far from the truth. The Bible describes hades as well as its successor, hell, as real place of "deep anguish", "eternal fire", and "eternal punishment" (Job 24:19, 26:5; Matthew 25:41, 46). We saw this in the example Jesus told of the rich man who went to hades who cried out in agony and asked the former beggar he knew to help quench his thirst (Luke 16:19–31). Yes, hades is a real place of suffering, agony, and misery.

- Much like heaven, hades is not a meta-physical state or an abstract notion, but rather a literal place where people who reject or rebel against God will go. From the example of the rich man and Lazarus, we can conclude that both people were fully conscious after their deaths—they understood their environments and were able to communicate with others. They also had human-like characteristics and emotions including feelings, memory, concern for others, and pain. Furthermore, the rich man was fully aware of the reason he was in hades and understood that his destiny was irrevocably fixed (Luke 16:26–28).

- The most important characteristic of hades is that God will not be present there. People who have rejected Christ and God's gift of salvation will spend eternity apart from God.

Tartarus

Tartarus is only mentioned once in the Bible (2 Peter 2:4). It is described as a dungeon of sorts for a special group of angels who sinned grievously against God by sleeping with women on earth prior to the great flood in the days of Noah (Genesis 6:1–4, Jude 6).

Tartarus is a special holding place for these fallen angels until their final judgment by God. It is not hell, but rather a separate and distinct place created for the special purpose of containing these fallen angels. Obviously, other demons and fallen angels are still free to move about and do Satan's will.

The Abyss / super crazy)

'The Abyss' is a phrase used in scripture to refer to a place of confinement for demons. It is separate from Tartarus as well as from hades and the lake of fire. Apparently, it is a place God can simply choose to banish evil spirits to at will—a jail of sorts or place of exile that only God has the key to. When Jesus was on earth, he came across a man possessed by literally thousands of demons (Luke 8:26–36). When Jesus confronted these demons, the Bible says they repeatedly begged Him not to order them to go into the Abyss. Apparently, these demons were very familiar with the Abyss and whatever torments would await them there. Instead, the demons begged Jesus to let them go into a herd of pigs nearby. Jesus, showing His mercy, allowed this.

The Bible doesn't state how evil spirits are banished to the Abyss or how many there are, but we do know that during the Tribulation period (a seven-year period that occurs just prior to Christ's return) the Abyss will be opened to release swarms of demonic creatures upon the earth (Revelation 9:1–10). When the Abyss is opened, smoke will rise from it which the Bible says will darken the sun and sky. This seems to confirm that the Abyss is a physical place and not just a symbolic reference or abstract notion. The Bible goes on to state that these demonic creatures who come out of the Abyss will follow a king who rules over them named "Abaddon" (in Hebrew) or "Apollyon" (in Greek). This king is described as "the angel of the Abyss" (Revelation 9:11). From this we can conclude that the Abyss has some form of hierarchical rule with a leader that lords over the evil spirits who reside there.

After Christ returns following the Tribulation period, the Bible states that Satan himself will be banished to the Abyss for the thousand-year period known as the Millennium (Revelation 20:1–3), after which he will be released for a short time. When the heavens and the earth are destroyed following the Millennium, the Abyss will be destroyed as well, along with all of God's 'old creation' and will be replaced by God's 'new creation' where all beings will spend eternity.

New Heaven/New Earth

The 'new heaven' and the 'new earth' is described extensively in the Bible. This is the place where all believers will spend eternity with God. It should be noted before going further that I'm using a singular pronoun because the "new heaven" and the "new earth" are essentially one in the same—unlike our world today where heaven and earth are two different places which have their own distinct identities, the new heaven and the new earth will basically be one creation without any boundary lines between them (Isaiah 65:17–18; Revelation 21:1–8). It is for this reason that I'll use the phrase "the eternal state" synonymously with the phrase "the new heaven and the new earth".

The eternal state does not exist today—it has yet to be created. After the Millennium, the Bible says that God will destroy the existing heavens and the earth and all that is in them with fire (Revelation 21:1; 2 Peter 3:7, 10, 12; Zephaniah 3:8). This destruction of the earth will be accompanied by a great noise—quite literally "a big bang" (2 Peter 3:10). He will then create a 'new heaven' and a 'new earth'—everything from prior creation will be wiped clean and recreated from new (Revelation 21:5; 2 Peter 3:10). In essence, God will start creation all over again just as He did "In the beginning" when He "created the heaven and the earth" the first time around (Genesis 1:1).

Why would God do this? Why would he start from scratch and create all of creation all over again? The answer is because of a rebellion rooted in our own sin. At the end of the Millennium, the Bible states that even after one thousand years of peace on earth under Christ's perfect rule, Satan will be freed and will lead countless numbers of people in one final rebellion. The Bible states that these people will "march across the breadth of the earth and surround the camp of God's people, the city He loves [a reference to Jerusalem]" at which point God will destroy these people with fire (Revelation 20:9). What's interesting to note is what this verse seems to imply—namely, that even after personally living with Christ on earth and experiencing the wonderful blessings of His Millennial Kingdom, apparently the vast majority of people on the earth will march against Jesus and encircle what appears to be the final holdout for believers—the city of Jerusalem. *Do all believers end up in Jerusalem?*

wow

This is difficult to imagine. How could people who have personally experienced Christ's presence and leadership revolt in such great numbers? Apparently, mankind is inherently sinful, prideful, and rebellious—and given the proper motivation (Satan in this instance), they will continue to reject and rebel against God. It is because of this the Bible states God will 'cleanse' the earth just as He did in the days of Noah. In those days the Bible says, "The Lord saw how great man's wickedness on the earth had become and that every inclination of the thoughts of his heart was only evil all the time." As a result, "The Lord was grieved that He had made man on the earth, and His heart was filled with pain" (Genesis 6:5–6). It was then that God decided to destroy His own creation with a flood and start again with Noah and his family. The destruction of the heavens and the earth following Satan's final rebellion will be similar—the people of the earth will apparently have shown just how evil they could become and the Lord will be filled with pain just as He was in the days of Noah. He will then proceed to destroy creation and start over gain— except this time He will destroy (or 'baptize') the earth by fire instead of by water, and instead of starting with just one family, He will start with all those who have accepted Him throughout the course of time.

Many people confuse this eternal state with Christ's Kingdom on earth. Although similar in some ways, they are actually quite different. The key difference between Christ's Kingdom as it will exist during the Millennium and this new creation will be that God will rule instead of Christ, and Christ's Kingdom will be limited in time to 1,000 years while the Eternal State will last forever. The Bible says that Jesus will "hand over His Kingdom to God" (1 Corinthians 15:24–28), who will interact with mankind at a personal level in this new creation just as Christ did during the Millennial Kingdom. In essence, the Millennium will just foreshadow what life will be like in the eternal state. Although the Millennium will be very different from the world as it stands today, it will still fall short of the perfection and glory that will exist in the eternal state with God.

What will the eternal state be like? Fortunately, unlike heaven and hades, the Bible provides quite a bit of detail. We know the following:

- God will personally live with mankind. He will be physically present and will interact with people face to face just as Jesus did during the time He ministered on earth during the first century and as He will during the Millennium (1 John 3:2; 1 Revelation 21:3, 22:4). This will represent a restoration of the original way God created us in the Garden of Eden—pure, in an ideal setting, and able to walk with God and interact with Him just as we would any other person.

- The name of God will be present "on everyone's foreheads" (Revelation 22:4). It's unclear if this is a figurative reference to everyone knowing God or a literal reference, but it's clear that there will be no unbelievers in the new creation (Revelation 21:8, 27).

- There will be no sin in the eternal state, for all the powers of evil (including Satan) will have been expelled to the lake of fire forever (Revelation 21:8).

Lovely (handwritten margin note)

- Eternity will be a time of immense joy. The Bible states that there will be no death, mourning, crying, or pain (Revelation 21:4). The eternal state will be a place of great joy and emotional peace. That's not to say that people won't grieve over lost friends and family who are in hell, but that God will help everyone understand His purposes and He'll comfort us in ways we don't quite understand. Our knowledge will be complete, and we will for the first time understand His ways. Jonathan Edwards once said that heaven will have no pity for hell, not because the saints are unloving, but because they are perfectly loving. We will for the first time be able to see everything in conformity with God's love, justice, and glory.

- There will be no hunger or thirst (Revelation 7:16). Our eternal bodies will not need nourishment on an ongoing basis as they do today, so the problems of malnutrition and starvation will no longer exist. ✱ Will we eat or celebrate around food?

- There will be no marriage (Matthew 22:29–30; 1 Corinthians 7:29–31). Although we will have individual identities and be able recognize, spend time, and interact with others as we wish, the human bonds of matrimony don't extend into eternity—they truly are only "until death do us part". This only makes sense given many problems with the human institution at it exists today including a divorce rate (at least in the United States) now slightly over 50%, multiple marriages being common place, polygamy and arranged marriages still existing in many cultures.

- There will be no sea (Revelation 21:1). It's not clear why this is, other than that the new creation will be so completely different than the existing creation that elements such as water and land will most likely be unnecessary. An alternative explanation is that the word 'sea' frequently stands for the nations of the world, and this might mean that the strife between rebellious nations and the turmoil that accompanies these struggles will vanish.

The capital city and the dwelling place for all believers in eternity will be known as the 'New Jerusalem'. The Bible provides quite a bit of detail about this place as well. In fact, this is the place that Christ said He was preparing for us when He said, "In my Father's house are many rooms; if it were not so, I would have told you. I am going there to prepare a place for you. And if I go and prepare a place for you, I will come back and take you to be with me that you also may be where I am" (John 14:2–3). Think of it—this is the place that Jesus has been preparing for at least the past two thousand years. Without discounting the ability for Christ to create the New Jerusalem with simply the words of His mouth, this is very likely what Jesus is in heaven doing today—building this city and preparing it for the arrival of His Church. Jesus, interestingly a carpenter by occupation while on earth, has told us that He has gone to undertake a construction project and at some point will come back and hold an open house and welcome us into our eternal mansions! How wonderful that will be.

Love it

The city itself will exist for all eternity and will be the final dwelling place for all believers (Revelation 3:12, 21–22). We know the following about this city:

- The throne of God and of Christ will be in the city (Revelation 22:3).

- There will be no Temple in the New Jerusalem, because the Lord God and Jesus will be its Temple (Revelation 21:22).

- There will be no night and day or need for the sun, moon or light because the Glory of God and Jesus will provide light for the Kingdom (Revelation 21:11, 23, 25, 22:5).

- The city itself will be laid out as a cube (or perhaps even a pyramid) with each side measuring 1,380 miles in length (Revelation 21:16–17). This would calculate to a base area roughly two-thirds the size of the continental United States with a height that would be the equivalent of 396,000 stories. It has been calculated that even if only 25 percent of this space were used for living space, 20 billion people could be accommodated with plenty of room.

- The city and streets of the New Jerusalem will be made of pure gold.

- The city will have a great, high wall around it. This wall will be 72 yards thick and will be made of jasper (Revelation 21:17–18, 21:21b). This wall will have twelve gates:
  - ➤ There will be three gates on each side of the city (North, South, East and West—Revelation 21:12–13).
  - ➤ Angels will be stationed at each of the gates (Revelation 21:12).
  - ➤ Each gate will be made of a single pearl (Revelation 21:21). This is where the phrase the "pearly gates" of heaven came from.   _interesting_
  - ➤ On the twelve gates will be written the names of the twelve tribes of Israel (Revelation 21:12).
  - ➤ The gates of the city will never be shut (Revelation 21:25).

- The wall of the city will have twelve foundations:
  - ➤ On these will be written the names of the twelve apostles of Christ (Revelation 21:14).
  - ➤ The foundations will be decorated with every kind of precious stone (jasper, sapphire, chalcedony, emerald, sardonyx, carnelian, chrysolite, beryl, topaz, chryoprase, jacinth, and amethyst—Revelation 21:19–20).

It seems odd, doesn't it, that the eternal dwelling place for all believers would be gated community. Why would such a wall, gates and sentinel angels be necessary? Won't the New Jerusalem just be surrounded by clouds that we can play on? The reason for the wall and gates is because "outside are the dogs, those who practice magic arts, the sexually immoral, the murderers, the idolaters, and everyone who loves and practices falsehood" (Revelation 22:15). Apparently, in the new creation, not only will the boundary between heaven and the earth be blurred, but so too will the boundary line between the dwelling of believers and the dwelling of unbelievers. In fact, this verse makes it appear that the New Jerusalem itself will exist as a shining city of wonderful blessings surrounded by the lake of fire where unbelievers will spend eternity. If this is the case, imagine the imagery—the New Jerusalem will quite literally be a place of wonders with no pain, hunger, thirst and where everyone will have a direct and personal relationship with God. However, outside will be a place of enormous torment where those that have chosen to reject God will forever be outside the walls with no opportunity to ever come in. These unbelievers will be reminded on a daily basis as they look at their fate and see the wonderful New Jerusalem in the distance, what the eternal consequence was for rejecting God and choosing to live apart from Him forever. *very sad ☹*

The Lake of Fire

The 'lake of fire' is synonymous with what most people think of as hell. It has been prepared by God as the ultimate residence for Satan and all the people of the world who have rejected God. It is described in the Bible as a literal place—a 'fiery lake of burning sulfur' where people will be 'tormented day and night forever and ever' where the 'fire never goes out' (Matthew 25:41; Mark 9:43, 48; Revelation 19:20, 20:10, 14–15). It certainly is no place that anyone would want to spend eternity. The lake of fire does not exist today. It will be created after the Millennium along with the new heaven and the new earth after God destroys the current heaven, earth, and hades. At this time, the Bible says that God will empty hades and send these unbelievers to the lake of fire. It is here where unbelievers will spend eternity. (1 Peter 3:18–19; Luke 16:19–31).

In the New Testament, the word 'gehenna' is used for hell. This word is actually derived from the Hebrew 'valley of Hinnom' found in the Old Testament (Joshua 15:8; 2 Kings 23:10; Nehemiah 11:30).

What's interesting about this is that it is a physical place—a real valley outside of Jerusalem where Jews at one point sacrificed humans to pagan gods. It was also a garbage dump for the city of Jerusalem during the time of Christ. As a result, the valley of Hinnom was a dirty, disgusting, worm infested place. This is why Christ referred to hell as the place where "their worm does not die, and the fire is not quenched" (Mark 9:44, 46, 48). He was making a reference to this valley of filth and disgust where pagan worship once took place. What's more, Christ may have been making a reference to the New Jerusalem as well. We saw in the previous section that "the dogs and the sorcerers and the immoral persons and the murderers and the idolaters, and everyone who loves and practices lying" will live outside the city walls (Revelation 21:15). So, just as the valley of Hinnom was a dirty and disgusting place for pagan worshipers outside the city walls of Jerusalem in ancient days, so too the lake of fire might very well be a horrible place of existence for unbelievers outside of the walls of the New Jerusalem in eternity.

What will the lake of fire be like? As mentioned before, it will be a literal lake of burning sulfur (Isaiah 33:14; Matthew 13:41–42; Mark 9:48; Revelation 14:10, 20:15) where there will be no rest (Luke 16:27) and where people will scream out for a single drop of water (Luke 16:24). It will also be a place of tremendous grief and despair. The Bible describes it as a "place of sorrows" (Psalm 18:5), where people "weep and wail" (Matthew 8:12, 13:42) and cry out for mercy (Luke 16:24). Despite the fire itself, hell will be a place of "blackness and darkness" (Jude 13). Unlike hades, though, there is no mention of people being able to communicate between heaven and hell in eternity, although the Bible does teach that Christ and the angels will be able to see those who are tormented (Revelation 14:10). This would be consistent with the description of the wall separating those in the New Jerusalem from those outside of its gates.

Awful

Some believe that Satan and his demons will torment the people who end up in hell. This is actually not the case. Although Satan and his demons will be present in hell, the Bible teaches that they will be among the tormented—they will not be the tormentors (Revelation 20:10).

There is no question that hell will be an absolutely terrible place. The imagery provided in the Bible defies imagination and belief, but the passages they are presented in describe hell in quite literal terms as opposed to figurative. Hell will indeed be just as horrible as it is described.

IF HEAVEN IS ALL JOY THEN WHY WILL WE KNOW & POTENTIALLY SEE THE TORMENT OUTSIDE THE GATED WALL?

HOW COULD GOD CREATE HELL?

The concept of the lake of fire, and eternal punishment in general, are difficult concepts for many to grasp. Some feel that the lake of fire couldn't actually exist—it just sounds too horrible to be taken literally. Others wonder how a loving God could create such a horrible place of eternal torture and pain where literally billions of people will sentenced to spend eternity. It does sound rather draconian, doesn't it? Does eternal punishment really fit the crime of unbelief while on earth? It is because of these questions that the modern Church has frequently ignored discussing the topic of hell altogether. Can you think of the last time that you actually heard a sermon describing the nature of hell? The topic is so undesirable to contemplate that it quite literally has driven many away from Christianity altogether. As a result, many denominations have watered down their teaching of hell to the point where millions of people now believe in some form of an afterlife, but one of eternal happiness for everyone, not of happiness for some and misery for others as the Bible teaches. Fear of hell has been replaced by a more appealing message for marketing reasons! Still others have tried to either take the hell out of forever (teaching that all people will eventually be in heaven even if some have to temporarily spend some time in hell) or have tried to take the forever out of hell (teaching that only Christians will live eternally, while the souls of unbelievers will simply be destroyed).

Unfortunately, these alternative views are not biblical and certainly were not what Jesus taught while He was on earth. In fact, out of the twelve times the word hell (gehenna) is used in the New Testament, eleven times it came directly from the mouth of Jesus. In fact, Jesus spoke more about hell during His ministry on earth than He did about heaven itself! Clearly, Jesus was trying to communicate not only the importance of being aware of hell, but also the consequences for those who would fail to take heed of His message.

But how could this be? How could God be all-loving and yet still allow eternal punishment? How could God create such a terrible place as hell? How could sentencing people to hell be a just punishment for unbelievers? Doesn't this make God appear cruel, vindictive, and grossly unfair? These are difficult questions to answer, but the Bible does provide some basic answers.

First, nobody will end up in hell by accident. In fact, God was so concerned with mankind that He sent His only son to die a very painful death in order to save us from this fate (John 3:16). Everyone has the opportunity to receive Christ and the pardon that His death provided. Author Tim LaHaye, in his book *Understanding the Last Days*, tells a story that brings this point to life:[1]

> In the archives of the Supreme Court of the United States is the record of a very strange incident that took place during the term of President Andrew Jackson. A man named George Wilson was sentenced to die by hanging for a crime he had committed. Somehow the story came before the President, who granted Wilson a pardon. To everyone's amazement, Wilson tore the pardon to shreds and threw it on the floor of his prison cell. The ensuing legal argument concerned the validity of a pardon that was refused, and the question arose as to whether or not Wilson should be freed or hanged. After great deliberation, the U.S. Supreme Court ruled as follows: "A pardon is a writing, the value of which is dependent upon the acceptance by the individual for who it is intended." It was therefore decreed by the court that George Wilson be hanged until dead—not because a pardon was not offered, but because it was not accepted.

---

[1] Tim LaHaye, *Understanding the Last Days*, p. 198

This is a perfect picture of the sinner who hears the gospel of Jesus Christ and knows that God has written a pardon for him, yet rejects Him and thus forfeits his right to the pardon.

Not to belittle it, but the 'Gospel message' that Christ instructed His disciples to preach around the world is essentially advertising of the fact that anyone in the world can receive a reprieve or pardon from this sentence of eternal punishment by simply accepting the pardon that Christ has already provided.

Second, although hell sounds grossly unjust when we hear of it, we should really ask about the nature of justice itself. Many people reject Christianity because they wonder how an all-powerful God could allow war, terrorism, rape, murder, and various other injustices to exist in the world. In fact, in most entry-level college philosophy courses, students are taught that the following three basic premises could not all be true, namely that 1) God is all-powerful, 2) God is all-loving and 3) there is evil in the world. The logic goes that if God were all-powerful and all-loving, then He would not allow evil in the world. Therefore, God is either not all-powerful (He does not have the power to restrain evil) or He is not all loving and doesn't care for His creation. There are many problems with this logic, including God's decision to give us free will and the result of original sin. However, in the context of this article, the point is that we can't have it both ways. We can't fault God for allowing evil to exist in the world and then turn around and fault Him for finally bringing justice to the world. There is war, terrorism, rape, murder, and other heinous injustices in the world; and God cannot allow these injustices to go unpunished.

How can a loving God allow hell to exist? Perhaps the real question should be: How can a loving God not allow hell to exist? God will bring final justice to the world and punishment to evildoers—would it not be inconsistent for Him to do otherwise? Could an all-loving and powerful God allow these injustices to continue forever? No— for God to be consistent with who He is, He must eventually punish the wicked for their sins. Fortunately, God has already paid the penalty for these sins. Author and evangelist Cliff Knechtle brings this point to life with a real story from his book *Give Me an Answer*:

> Two close friends graduated from college in Australia. One became a judge and the other a banker. One day the banker was arrested for embezzlement of one million dollars. He was to be tried before his friend. There was great speculation in the press. Would the judge throw the book at his buddy, proving what a just judge he was? Or would he let his friend off free? The courtroom was packed. The jury deliberated. They delivered the verdict—guilty. The judge then gave the sentence. He leveled the harshest fine possible against his friend.
>
> The crowd gasped in amazement. But then everyone watched in wonder as the judge stood, took off his robe, walked around the bar, and extended his hand to his friend. He said, "I have sold my house, taken all my savings out of my account. I have paid the fine I just leveled against you."
>
> The judge was just and the judge was loving. Justice was honored. But friendship was honored too. And all in the one act of paying the fine. That is how it works with Christ's death on the cross. In one act, both justice and love are found. God cannot turn His back on sin. He cannot ignore it. But the penalty for our sin was paid by his Son's death. And He cannot ignore that either. All he asks us to do is accept it.

So how could a loving God create hell? Because He must to be consistent with His character. However, also consistent with His character, He has provided a pardon for us to avoid this fate—all we have to do is simply accept it.

WHAT BEINGS EXIST IN THE SPIRIT WORLD?

It is natural when studying the spirit world and the nature of heaven and hell to ask what other type of beings actually exist out there. We've already seen several, which perhaps are new to many, including those that cohabitated with woman on earth prior to the flood and others which are imprisoned in the Abyss. What other types of beings exist?

The truth is that mankind is by no means alone in the universe! It's interesting that all sorts of movies, books, and TV shows center on this theme and explore UFO sightings, alien encounters, and life on other planets. Mankind seems to have an inherent need to know if we are all there is or if other beings exist out there somewhere. Fortunately, we need look no further than the Bible. Although the Bible doesn't speak directly to life on other planets, it certainly does give us a clear picture of a variety of other beings that exist in God's creation. Before exploring these, it's important to point out that all of these beings were in fact, created by God Himself—there is no separate creation independent from God. Colossians 1:16 says "For by Him all things were created: things in heaven and on earth, visible and invisible, whether thrones or powers or rules or authorities; all things were created by Him and for Him."

Angels

Most people are familiar with angels. We place images of them in our nativity scenes and on top of our trees at Christmas. Pictures of them appear in famous pieces of art and in many Bibles. We have even had a TV show about them *(Touched by an Angel)* to remind us of their existence. But what are angels really like and what does the Bible actually say about them? Fortunately, we know a great deal. The existence of angels is taught in at least thirty-four books of the Bible and the word 'angel' itself appears about 275 times in Scripture. Christ Himself taught of their existence (Matthew 18:10, 26:53). So, what are they like? We know the following:

- They are spirit beings who do not die (Hebrews 1:14; Luke 20:26). They are not humans. Some think that angels are simply believers who have passed away and gone on to heaven, but this is not the case. Angels are a separate species that were created by God distinct from human beings (Psalm 8:4–5). They were created before the creation of the earth (Job 38:6–7) and will live for eternity.

- There are "innumerable" numbers of them (Hebrews 12:22 KJV; Revelation 5:11).

- They are powerful (2 Thessalonians 1:7). In fact, the Bible says that one angel destroyed 185,000 soldiers of the Assyrian army in a night. Another rolled away the stone from the Tomb of Christ, which likely weighed between one and a half to two tons and we are told that one angel will bind Satan and cast him into the Abyss (Revelation 20:1–3). Clearly, angels have great strength, but they are not all-powerful as God is.

- All of the angels mentioned in Scripture are men (with the one possible exception being Zechariah 5:9, which is not conclusive). They do not marry and do not have the ability to procreate amongst themselves (Matthew 22:30). However, they can have sex as evidenced by the fact that some had intercourse with the "daughters of men" prior to the flood which resulted in a unique race of exceptional people (Genesis 6:1–4).

- They can clearly sin as evidenced by the previous point as well as the account of the original rebellion led by Satan against God.

- They have emotions much like our own including intellect (1 Peter 1:12), joy (Luke 2:13), and free will (Jude 6).

- They can view and observe the events of those on earth (1 Corinthians 4:9; 1 Timothy 5:21).

- Their primary purpose is to be "ministering spirits sent to serve those who will inherit salvation" (Hebrews 1:13–14). Their principle function is actually to minister to us—humans on earth who are believers in Christ! This includes serving as guardian angels for children (Matthew 18:10) as well as for adults (Genesis 48:16; Psalm 91:11; Acts 12:15). Examples of this role includes freeing Peter from prison (Acts 12:7), encouraging him when he had to stand trial (Acts 27:23–24), and caring for believers upon death (Luke 16:22; Jude 9).

  Great news!

- In addition to ministering to believers, angels also perform other tasks for God. This included assisting Christ. They made announcements concerning His coming (Luke 1:26–33; 2:9–15), physically protected and strengthened Him while on earth (Matthew 2:13, 4:11, 26:53, 22:43), and assisted in His ministry (Matthew 28:2, 28:6). They announce pending judgments (Genesis 19:13; Revelation 14:6–7) and inflict punishment (Acts 12:23). They will bring final judgment to the world during the Tribulation period (2 Thessalonians 1:7–8; Revelation 7:1–3, 8–19, 15–16), gather the body of believers from around the world after Christ's return (Matthew 24:31), and capture Satan following the Tribulation period (Revelation 20:1–4).

From the various passages on angels that exist in the Bible, we know that the spirit world is organized hierarchically, much like human society today. The Bible states that there are "rulers and authorities in the heavenly realms" (Ephesians 3:10). This makes sense, since it is consistent with the various passages in the Bible that discuss the eternal rewards for mankind in Christ's Kingdom (discussed later in this article), which includes the ability for different people to rise to different positions of power and authority depending upon their service and faithfulness on earth.

Michael

Michael is given the title of 'archangel' in the Bible (Jude 9). He is described as "the great prince" (Daniel 12:1) and the commander of the angelic army of heaven (Revelation 12:7–9). Angels are organized hierarchically and Michael is their leader (or at least one of them). If God were to have a cabinet like the President of the United States, Michael would be equivalent to the defense secretary or chairman of the Joint Chiefs—he's in charge of the military. In this role, Michael is seen to be Satan's primary adversary. Michael will lead the battle and triumph over Satan in the last days (Revelation 12:7–9) and has rescued other angels who were locked in fights with Satan's forces (Daniel 10:13). Michael has also fought verbally with Satan—Jude 9 describes a dispute they had regarding Moses. Clearly Satan and Michael interact with one another and view each other as rivals or enemies.

Michael is also described in the Bible as a special guardian of the affairs of Israel (Daniel 12:1). The Bible says he "protects" the people and the nation from supernatural forces. Furthermore, Michael will be given the role of announcing the rapture (an event when believers in Christ will be taken to heaven—1 Thessalonians 4:16). Michael certainly has important responsibilities in the spirit world. He can be considered God's "go-to guy" for important tasks.

(handwritten margin note: only 2 named in scripture)

Gabriel

Gabriel is God's messenger. He is not ranked as highly as Michael, but his position is certainly significant. He "stands in the presence of God" (Luke 1:19) and is sent out to deliver important messages on God's behalf. These messages included the interpretation of dreams for Daniel as well as pregnancy announcements for Zechariah and Joseph. Gabriel is mentioned four times (Daniel 8:16, 9:21–22; Luke

1:19, 26) and is the only angel besides Michael who is personally named in the Bible. To continue the cabinet analogy, Gabriel would be the equivalent of God's press secretary.

Seraphs

In the strictest sense, Seraphs are not angels—they are a different species of spirit beings. Perhaps they can be considered a different order of angelic beings, but they have a different form and function than Michael, Gabriel, and the angels previously described. The Bible only mentions them once and in this instance, they are seen as agents of cleansing who facilitate the worship of God. They are described as having a human-like form (including faces, hands and feet) as well as six wings (Isaiah 6:1–7).

Cherubim

Cherubim are yet another species, or order, of spirit beings. They are described as being God's guardians. God placed cherubim with swords to guard the way to the tree of life in the Garden of Eden (Genesis 3:24) and a representation of them was crafted on top of the Ark of the Covenant to symbolize the guarding of God's 'seat' or presence (Exodus 25:18–22). If the archangel Michael is in charge of the military, then perhaps the cherubim can be considered God's secret service agents.

Cherubim are described to be very quick—"like flashes of lightning", and have somewhat of a human form including legs and hands, as well as two pairs of wings. However, there are other differences. Cherubim are described to have four faces on their heads (the front like a man, the right side like a lion, the left side like an ox and the back like an eagle) and their feet are described to be "like those of a calf" (Ezekiel 1:4–14). Clearly, cherubim are a combination of human, angelic, and animal forms.

Satan

Satan is very real. Although to many he may seem like a caricature or a representation of evil in general, the Bible is clear that he is indeed a real creature (Ezekiel 28:14). His existence is taught in seven Old Testament books and by every New Testament writer. Jesus Himself stated that He had seen Satan (Luke 10:18) and taught of his existence (Matthew 13:39; Luke 11:18). Like the other beings of the spirit world, Satan has human-like qualities. He has emotions (Revelation 12:17), intelligence (2 Corinthians 11:3), and free will (2 Timothy 2:26). He has certainly sinned (1 John 3:8). The Bible says he has lied (John 8:44), murdered (John 8:44), and rebelled against God (Isaiah 14:13–14).

Unlike Michael and Gabriel, Satan was a cherub. Ezekiel 28:12–17 says that he was originally ordained by God to be a guardian cherub—responsible for protecting the throne of God. He was described as a "model of perfection, full of wisdom and perfect in beauty", "blameless" in his ways. Unfortunately though, Satan became prideful because of his physical beauty. This led him to believe he could be equal with God (Isaiah 14:13–14). The Bible says he became "filled with violence" and that he sinned by rebelling against God. As a result, God drove him in disgrace from His presence and expelled him to earth as a spectacle before the other spirit beings.

whoa!?!

To use the cabinet analogy, Satan was in charge of the secret service (God's chief cherub) while Michael was in charge of the military. In this role, Satan attempted a coup because he viewed himself as powerful as God. The coup attempt failed and Satan, as well as the other people who plotted against God, were expelled from the kingdom. Today, Satan continues to wage battle against the armies of God with Michael continuing to be Satan's biggest adversary. The Bible states that Satan will continue to wage war in the spirit world and on earth today, throughout the end times, and even near the end of the Millennium (Christ's kingdom on earth). Satan will not give

names for Satan

up, but will eventually be banished to the lake of fire along with everyone else who has rejected God (Revelation 20:10).

In the Bible, Satan is given many names. He is called the devil, Lucifer, Beelzebub (Matthew 12:24) and Belial (2 Corinthians 6:15). He's also called the evil one (1 John 5:19), the tempter (1 Thessalonians 3:5), the prince of this world (John 12:31), God of this age (2 Corinthians 4:4), ruler of the kingdom of the air (Ephesians 2:2), and the accuser of the brethren of Christ (Revelation 12:10).

Demons

Demons are spirit beings (Matthew 17:18). They are described as angels (Revelation 12:7). As such, they are not simply humans or "bad people" who have passed away and gone onto Hades, but rather a separate species of beings that were created by God distinct from the human race (Psalm 8:4–5). Satan is given the name "prince of demons" (Matthew 12:24), indicating that he is their leader in a hierarchical society similar to how the angels, cherubim, and seraphs relate to God. The Bible doesn't specifically state that demons are the angels who rebelled against God in Satan's original coup attempt, but many assume this and it's certainly the most logical explanation of who they are.

The demon world is well organized. They are described as being at war with God and mankind with the primary objectives of deceiving mankind, leading them astray (Ephesians 6:10–12; 1 Timothy 4:1–3), and thwarting the will of God (Daniel 10:10–14).

Demons are intimately familiar with the nature of the spirit world and of God. They know who Jesus is and, in fact, acknowledged Him as "the Holy One of God" (Mark 1:24) and the "Son of God" (Matthew 8:24) when Christ confronted some on earth. They are also said to know His plan for salvation (James 2:19) and their eventual fate, which is to be cast with Satan in the lake of fire for eternity (Matthew 8:29; 25:41).

Some demons are currently confined in Tartarus and the Abyss (2 Peter 2:4; Jude 6), while others are free to do Satan's work. The ones that are confined include those that cohabitated with women prior to the Flood as well as various others whom God chose to imprison there.

Demon possession is real. One or many demons can reside inside of a person and directly influence the actions of that individual. This is different from just influencing or tempting people from the outside. With possession, demons directly influence and direct the actions of individuals from the inside. Demon possession includes the ability to inflict sickness, blindness, dumbness, muteness, insanity, suicidal mania, personal injuries, supernatural strength, and physical defects and other deformities upon people (Matthew 9:32–33, 12:22, 15:22; Mark 9:18–22; Luke 4:35, 8:26–36, 9:42, 13:11–17). The Bible says that demons can posses people and come and go at will (Luke 11:24–26), but fortunately, Christians cannot be possessed by a demon since Christians have the Holy Spirit inside of them that protects believers from this.

WHAT WILL OUR BODIES BE LIKE IN ETERNITY?

Almost all religions around the world promise their followers a spiritual resurrection of some kind where the 'spirit' or 'soul' of a person lives on into an afterlife, but this is where Christianity is different. What makes Christianity unique is that both the Old and New Testament speak of a bodily resurrection for all people—where the spirit of a person is physically reunited with a form of their former physical body. This body won't be the same body that we know of (which may have been destroyed, cremated, or decayed), but rather a greatly improved version of their body that will last for eternity. This is true for both believers and unbelievers—at some point everyone's spirit will be rejoined with their physical body.

Christ is the primary example. When Christ died, His spirit was separated from His body; but when He was resurrected, His spirit was re-joined with His body, which was a glorified version of His former body. Although Christ's body was recognizable and similar in many ways to His previous body (Mark 16:9–10; John 20:18) and still held the scars of his crucifixion (John 20:26–28), it was also more than just physical because He had the power to walk through doors (John 20:19) and move from place to place seemingly at will. Likewise, our resurrected bodies will also have some physical properties and some supernatural properties. These bodies will:

- Be just like the one Christ had after His resurrection (1 John 3:2).

- Be glorified, improved versions of our existing earthly bodies (Philippians 3:21; 1 Corinthians 15:49).

- Be real, and will be able to see, feel, thirst, talk, and remember (Luke 16:19–31), but will not have physical limitations such as disease, aging, disability, or tragedy (1 Corinthians 15:35–50).

- Be capable of personal feelings, including joy, sorrow (Psalm 16:11; Revelation 7:17; 21:4), and a desire for justice (Revelation 6:9–10).

- Be recognizable and similar in appearance to our existing bodies (Matthew 8:11, 17:3–4; Luke 24:39). As a result, our personal relationships and knowledge of others will simply continue on into heaven and the depth of the relationships we have today will only increase in heaven (1 Corinthians 13:12). It's comforting to think that when we get to heaven, we'll actually be able to interact and spend time with those that we loved on earth in much the same way that we do today. People who have lost spouses, parents, grandparents, and other loved ones who were believers will truly be able to see them once again. Someone once said, "Will we know each other in heaven? The truth is that we won't really know each other *until* we get to heaven."

- Be able to travel effortlessly and not be subject to material forces (Luke 24:31–37; John 20:26). When Jesus was resurrected, he was able to appear to the disciples who were meeting behind locked doors, move from place to place seemingly at will, and disappear from their presence instantly. Clearly, our resurrected bodies won't be made of atomic matter the way they are today, but rather will be some combination of the physical and the spiritual.

- Be able to eat—we will be able to enjoy food just as we do today (Luke 22:17–18; John 21:10–15; Revelation 19:7). Having said that, the Bible states that there will be no hunger or thirst in God's Kingdom (Revelation 7:16), so obviously, our eternal bodies will not need the nourishment that food provides.

- Have gender. We will not marry in the afterlife (Matthew 22:29–30), but that doesn't mean that our bodies will be sexless. Given the examples in the Bible of angels having gender and Christ's form after His resurrection, it's safe to assume that our current gender will continue on into eternity.

Clearly, our resurrected bodies will be very similar to our current ones, but we also know that physical deformities won't exist in heaven, so as our bodies are raised, they will be made perfect by God. 1 Corinthians 15:42–44, 50 says:

> "So will it be with the resurrection of the dead. The body that is sown is perishable, it is raised imperishable; it is sown in dishonor, it is raised in glory; it is sown in weakness, it is raised in power; it is sown a natural body, it is raised a spiritual body...I declare to you brothers, that flesh and blood cannot inherit the kingdom of God, nor does the perishable inherit the imperishable."

How this happens exactly, we don't know, but whether a person was cremated or buried, healthy or handicapped, young or old, we will all be rejoined with some form of our physical bodies to spend eternity with God. These bodies will not be flesh and blood, but rather made of a substance that will last forever.

THE TRUTH ABOUT ETERNITY & THE SPIRIT WORLD

WHEN WILL WE RECEIVE OUR ETERNAL BODIES?

Although most people think of the word 'resurrection' as being synonymous with 'rising from the dead', this isn't exactly what is meant by this word in the Bible. When a person dies, their spirit is separated from their body, but this state is only temporary. At the time of a person's resurrection—and all people will be resurrected at some point—their spirit will be reunited with their physical body. This combination of a 'spirit' and an 'eternal body' is how all people will exist for eternity.

> "They [believers] came to life and reigned with Christ a thousand years. The rest of the dead did not come to life until the thousand years were ended. This is the first resurrection. Blessed and holy are those who have part in the first resurrection. The second death has no power over them." (Revelation 20:4–6)

When will these resurrections from the dead happen? There are actually five different times mentioned in the Bible when God will reunite the bodies of a group of people with their spirits. The Bible groups these and refers to them as two different resurrections—a first and a second. The first resurrection actually has several different phases to it and includes only believers in Christ. The second resurrection occurs at the end of the Millennium and is for unbelievers. As with the judgments of mankind (discussed later in this article), the timing of these bodily resurrections will occur at different times for different classes of people.

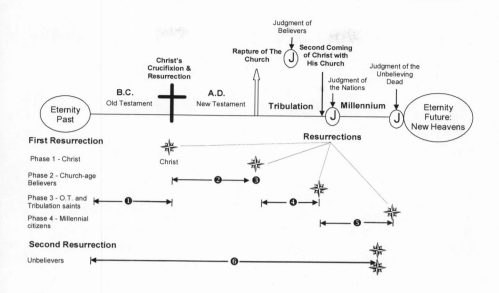

The First Resurrection					
Believers	**Died prior to Christ ❶**	**Died after Christ ❷**	**Alive during Rapture ❸**	**Died during Tribulation ❹**	**Alive at 2nd Coming ❺**
Where spirit goes after death:	Paradise; but taken to heaven with Christ at His resurrection	Heaven	No death; taken directly to heaven during Rapture	Heaven	No death; enter Millennium in physical bodies
Time of resurrection (i.e. given eternal body):	At Judgment of Nations	At Rapture	At Rapture	At Judgment of Nations	At end of Millennium
Status during the Millennium:	Eternal body	Eternal body	Eternal body	Eternal body	Physical body
Eternal destiny:	The Eternal State				

The Second Resurrection	
Unbelievers ❻	All Time
Where spirit goes after death:	Hades
Time of resurrection (i.e. given eternal body):	Judgment of the Unsaved Dead
Eternal destiny:	Lake of Fire

It should be noted that the second resurrection (the one for unbelievers) is also referred to in the Bible as the 'second death' (Revelation 20:14b). The first death for unbelievers will be when they physically die and go to hades. The second death will be when they are resurrected, judged, and sent to hell. For believers, there will be no second death. A simple poem that captures this concept is the following:

"He who is born but once, shall die twice; But he who is born twice shall die but once."

—*Hal Lindsey*

Being 'born twice', of course, refers to a believer's acceptance of Christ, which is commonly referred to as being 'born again'.

The First Resurrection

There are four phases to the first resurrection, or uniting of believers' spirits with their eternal bodies. This means that there are four distinct points in time when this uniting will occur. Different people will be resurrected at different times depending upon when they lived:

Phase 1—Christ: The Bible states that Jesus was the first 'believer' to be resurrected. He is called "the first-fruits of those who have fallen asleep" (1 Corinthians 15:20–25). When Christ died, His spirit was taken to paradise. When He rose from the dead, His spirit was re-joined with His physical body, which then walked the earth, interacted with people, and eventually ascended into heaven. Jesus still possesses his resurrected body in heaven, and the Bible says that at the time of His return, people will recognize Him and will be able to see the scars from His crucifixion (Zechariah 12:10; Revelation 1:7).

Phase 2—The Rapture: Whenever believers die, their spirits are immediately taken to heaven (2 Corinthians 5:8; Philippians 1:21–23). At the time of the Rapture, the bodies of those that have died will be resurrected and will be re-joined with their spirits in heaven. Believers who are alive at the time of the Rapture will be immediately changed and given their eternal bodies without ever dying. Both groups of people will then be taken to heaven (1 Corinthians 15:52).

Phase 3—Judgment of the Nations: When Christ returns, He will judge the people of the world at what is called the Judgment of the Nations. It is at this point that Old Testament saints and believers who were martyred during the Tribulation period will be resurrected and given their eternal bodies (Revelation 20:4; Daniel 12:1–2, 13; Isaiah 26:19).

Phase 4—Millennial Citizens: Believers who were alive at the time of the Second Coming will enter the Millennial kingdom in their physical, mortal bodies. They will live this way throughout the Millennium. It is only after the Millennium, when God destroys the world and creates a "new heaven and a new earth", that these believers will be given their eternal bodies.

The Second Resurrection

When unsaved people die, their spirits are immediately taken to hades. As discussed previously, hades is not hell. Rather, it is a temporary holding place for unbelievers (1 Peter 3:18–19). The second resurrection, which is for all unbelievers who've lived since the beginning of time, will occur after the Millennium. It is the point at which unbelievers will be re-joined with their bodies to stand before the throne of God for judgment (Revelation 20:11–15). This judgment is called the Judgment of the Unbelieving Dead. Unbelievers will be judged based on their works and will all be ultimately thrown into the lake of fire in their resurrected bodies for eternal punishment.

WHAT IS JUDGMENT DAY?

The term 'Judgment Day' is frequently used in modern day movies, songs and books. Mankind seems to intrinsically know that at the end of life, there will be a time of reckoning—a time when people will be accountable for the lives they've lived. It will be a time when the creator will bring everyone's 'accounts into balance' and reward those who are worthy of reward and punish those who are worthy of punishment. While most people are familiar with the concept, very few actually know what the Bible says about it.

Although most people hear the phrase "Judgment Day" and think of a single day or time of judgment, the Bible actually describes three different judgments that will occur to judge all the people of the world. In all cases, Christ will be the judge, but the timing of the judgments and the circumstances will be different for different types of people. There are many misconceptions of these judgments. Many believe that these judgments will be based on good deeds and that a person will not know his or her eternal status until Judgment Day. This is not the case. No person is good enough to meet God's standard (Romans 3:10–20). All have sinned (Romans 3:23). Instead, what will determine a person's eternal destiny will be his or her acceptance or rejection of Jesus Christ. This is a conscious choice that all people make during their lifetimes. The hope for believers at judgment day then, is not for an innocent verdict (since all are guilty), but rather for an acquittal through the grace of Jesus Christ. Those that rejected Christ's pardon during their lifetimes will have no basis to be found innocent and will ultimately be sentenced to eternal punishment.

The following is a summary of the three different judgments the Bible describes; the Judgment of Believers, the Judgment of the Nations and the Judgment of the Unsaved Dead:

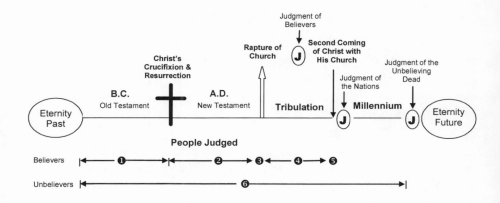

	Judgment of Believers	Judgment of the Nations	Judgment of the Unbelieving Dead
Nickname	Bema Seat Judgment	Sheep & Goats Judgment	Great White Throne Judgment
Key Scriptures	1 Corinthians 3:11–15; 2 Corinthians 5:10	Daniel 12:1–3; Joel 3:2; Ezekiel 20:34–38; Matthew 25:31–46; Revelation 20:4–6	Revelation 20:11–15; 2 Peter 3:7
Place	In heaven (before the 'Bema Seat' of Christ)	The 'Valley of Jehoshaphat'	Before the 'Great White Throne' of God
Judge	Christ	Christ	Christ
People Judged	❷❸: All believers in Christ prior to the Rapture (does not include Old Testament saints who lived prior to the First Coming of Christ)	❶❹❺: Old Testament saints, those martyred during the Tribulation, and all those living (both Jews and Gentiles) at time of Christ's Second Coming	❻: All unsaved people from the beginning of time, except those living at the time of Christ's Second Coming

Basis for Judgment	Salvation guaranteed. Additional rewards are determined based on a believer's works since time of salvation.	• O.T. Saints – faith in God • Believers who died during Tribulation – faith in Christ • Living Gentiles – faith in Christ as proved by how they treated Israel during Tribulation period • Living Jews – acceptance of Christ	Based on their rejection of the Messiah and their own works
Result	Rewards in heaven given or lost	• Saved ('sheep') – entrance into the Millennial Kingdom • Unsaved ('goats') – cast into Lake of Fire (i.e. hell)	All will be thrown into the Lake of Fire (i.e. hell)

Judgment of Believers

The first judgment will be the Judgment of Believers (also known as the Judgment of the Church or the 'Bema Seat' judgment). After the Church is raptured and taken to heaven, all believers in Christ will be judged. Salvation is not at risk, because the people who will have been raptured have already been selected as believers. What is at stake at this judgment, though, are rewards that Christ will give out based on a believer's deeds. 2 Corinthians 5:10 says "we will must all appear before the judgment seat of Christ, that each one may receive what is due him for the things done while in the body." This judgment isn't about the sins we've committed or the bad things we've done, but rather the good things we've done as Christians and the motives for doing them. This judgment will be an awards ceremony of sorts, where faithful and true believers will be recognized and rewarded by God.

The Judgment of Believers will include everyone who has put his or her faith in Jesus Christ and accepted His offer of salvation. This includes all believers in Christ throughout the ages—from the time of Christ's First Coming to the time of the Rapture. However, this judgment does not include Old Testament saints (those who believed in God prior to the First Coming of Christ such as Moses and the prophets). These people will not have been raptured with the Church, since the Rapture only includes those who "died in Christ" (1 Thessalonians 4:16). This later group will be judged as part of the Judgment of the Nations described below.

Christ will be the judge (2 Corinthians 5:10; John 5:22), and each person will be judged based on their deeds and what the motives were for these deeds since the time of their salvation. First Corinthians 3:13–15 says that on this day "[each man's] work will be shown for what it is, because the Day will bring it to light. It will be revealed with fire, and the fire will test the quality of each man's work. If what he has built survives, he will receive his reward. If it is burned up, he will suffer loss; he himself will be saved, but only as one escaping through the flames." Christ will be judging on this day the quality of each person's work to determine the appropriate reward— He will not only look at the work itself, but also the quality and lasting value of each deed. The word 'fire' in this parable is used figuratively as an indication that each person's deeds will be tested thoroughly.

What a person did before they were a Christian will not be considered nor are sins that were committed at any point in a believer's life. Many are fearful that when they get to heaven, everything they have done and every sin they have committed will be revealed to the world. Although this will, in fact, be the case for unbelievers, it will not be the case for believers. God assures believers that our "sins and lawless acts I will remember no more" (Hebrews 10:17). When Christ died for our sins, He once and for all paid the price for these sins. We need not worry about reliving them or having God accuse us again for what he has already forgiven us for.

Judgment of The Nations

The second judgment will be the Judgment of the Nations. This is the judgment most frequently referred to as "Judgment Day" by most people. The Judgment of the Nations will occur on earth immediately after the Second Coming of Christ. All people living at the end of the Tribulation period will be gathered together for judgment and their eternal destiny will be determined. This judgment is frequently referred to as the Sheep and Goats judgment based on a parable Jesus told; He said He would separate the "sheep from the goats":

> "When the Son of Man comes in His glory, and all the angels with Him, He will sit on His throne in heavenly glory. All the nations will be gathered before Him, and He will separate the people one from another as a shepherd separates the sheep from the goats. He will put the sheep on His right and the goats on His left. Then the King will say to those on His right, 'Come, you who are blessed by my Father; take your inheritance, the kingdom prepared for you since the creation of the world'…Then He will say to those on His left, 'Depart from me, you who are cursed, into the eternal fire prepared for the devil and his angels.'" (Matthew 25:31–34, 41)

Also included in this judgment will be all of the believers who were killed during the Tribulation period (Revelation 20:4) and all of the Old Testament saints (people who believed in God prior to the First Coming of Christ—Daniel 12:1–2, 13; Isaiah 26:19). The question is often asked, "Why are Old Testament saints and believers in Christ treated differently? Why aren't the Old Testament saints resurrected with Christians at the time of the Rapture and taken to heaven along with the Church prior to this judgment?" It would seem that making a distinction between 'believers in Christ' and 'believers in God' is arbitrary. The answer to this question is that there is a significant distinction between the two, and God has very different plans for Israel and for the Church. Prior to the First Coming of Christ, God's plan of salvation for people was different than it is today. Salvation

THE TRUTH ABOUT ETERNITY & THE SPIRIT WORLD

was based on belief in God, sacrificial offerings, and obedience to the law. This plan was primarily directed toward the Jews, and was based on the covenants God made with Abraham, Isaac, David, and Moses. When Christ came, He died as a sacrifice for sin. His death was a substitute for the sin offerings and obedience to the law required by God in the Old Testament. In essence, His death changed the rules, and now salvation is based solely on faith in Christ. Salvation today, although open to the Jews, is primarily directed towards Gentiles due to Israel's rejection of Christ at His First Coming. As such, the Old Testament Saints and the Church are treated differently by God, both in how they are judged, and the 'inheritance' that they will receive after His Second Coming.

At the end of the Tribulation period immediately following Armageddon, the Bible says Christ will gather all nations together for judgment in the 'Valley of Jehoshaphat' (Matthew 25:31–36; Ezekiel 20:33–38; Joel 3:2, 12; Zephaniah 3:8). Although there are several Jehoshaphats mentioned in the Bible, the exact location of the 'Valley of Jehoshaphat' is not known. Most likely, this reference is to the Kidron Valley, which is located between Jerusalem and the Mount of Olives.

As with the Judgment of Believers, Christ will be the judge (Matthew 25:31; John 5:22) for this one as well, although others will be given authority by Christ to judge and will help in the judging process (Revelation 20:4). Although the Bible doesn't say who these 'others' are (other than to mention that they "sit on thrones"), Christ promised his twelve disciples that they would "sit on twelve thrones, judging the twelve tribes of Israel" (Matthew 19:28; Luke 22:29–30) and promised that the Church would "judge the world" (1 Corinthians 6:2). As a result, it's probably safe to assume that people who were faithful in serving Christ and received significant recognition during the Judgment of Believers will be the ones given authority to help in this judgment. The criteria for judgment will be as follows:

- Gentiles who were living at the end of the Tribulation period will be judged based on how they treated the 144,000 Jews (which, during intense persecution, is evidence of their attitude toward God—Matthew 25:35–40; Joel 3:2–3).

- Jews who were living at the end of the Tribulation period will be judged based on their obedience to God and acceptance of Christ as the Messiah (Ezekiel 20:37–38; Daniel 12:1–2).

- Believers in Christ who died during the Tribulation period will be judged based on their faith in Jesus.

- Old Testament saints will be judged based on their faith in God and their obedience to Him.

Salvation is at risk and is the primary point of this judgment. People who pass judgment will enter the Millennial Kingdom, which Christ will establish following this judgment. They will then live with Christ for one thousand years on earth (Matthew 25:34, 46; Daniel 12:2, 13; Revelation 20:4, 6). Those who don't pass judgment will be cast immediately into the lake of fire for eternal punishment. These people will then be separated from the presence of the Lord forever (Matthew 25:41, 46; Daniel 12:2; 2 Thessalonians 1:8–9).

Judgment of the Unbelieving Dead

The third and final judgment is called the Judgment of the Unbelieving Dead. After the Millennium, Christ will resurrect and judge all of the unsaved people of the world who have died since the beginning of time (except those who were living at the end of the Tribulation period—those people will have already been judged and cast into the Lake of Fire as part of the Judgment of the Nations). This judgment is frequently referred to as 'the Great White Throne Judgment' based on the passage from Revelation where it is described:

"Then I [John] saw a great white throne and Him who was seated on it…And I saw the dead, great and small, standing before the throne, and books were opened…The sea gave up the dead that were in it, and death and hades gave up the dead that were in them, and each person was judged according to what he had done…If anyone's name was not found written in the book of life [list of those saved], he was thrown into the lake of fire." (Revelation 20:11–15)

Christ will be the judge (John 5:22). The result of this judgment is that all of these unsaved people will be thrown into the lake of fire forever—it will be a terrible time of despair and grief. Imagine the anguish that this judgment will bring as literally billions of people are judged only to suffer the same terrible fate of being sentenced to eternity in the Lake of Fire. What a horrible sight this will be, which begs the question, "Why must this judgment even happen? If everyone will suffer the same fate, why bother with the judgment? Why doesn't God just immediately throw everyone into the lake of fire?"

The answer to these questions relates to the nature of this judgment. The primary purpose is not to determine guilt or innocence (since all will be guilty of rejecting Christ), but rather to show the unbelievers at this judgment why they are being sentenced to such a terrible eternal fate. The Bible says that God is recording everyone's deeds in a book. These books will be opened during this judgment to reveal what each person had done (Revelation 20:12–12). Every sin that a person has committed will be brought before him so that he can see the wickedness of his ways. People will realize that they are not righteous. They are sinners and guilty of the punishment that will be handed down against them. Since they rejected the pardon that God gave (in the form of Jesus Christ), they will see that God (a God of justice) has no choice but to sentence them to this punishment.

It's at this judgment that all unbelievers will finally concede that Jesus Christ is the one true Lord, and will bow at the mention of His name (Philippians 2:9–11).

WHAT ARE ETERNAL REWARDS?

During the judgment of believers, we are told that Christ will judge our deeds and provide rewards to those that were faithful—that "each one may receive what is due him for things done while in the body" (2 Corinthians 5:10). But what are these rewards? How should we view them and what should our attitude be toward accumulating rewards?

Fortunately, when Christ was on earth, he taught extensively about eternal rewards. One of the most significant passages is in Matthew 6:19–20:

> "Do not lay up for yourselves treasures on earth, where moth and rust destroy and where thieves break in and steal; but lay up for yourselves treasures in heaven, where neither moth nor rust destroys and where thieves do not break in and steal."

In this passage, Christ is trying to convince us that His treasure—heavenly treasure—is far better to have than earthly treasure. Why? Because heavenly treasure will last forever, while earthly treasure will not. Looking deeper into this passage though, there are three other points we need to consider. The first is that Christ instructs us to 'lay up' or accumulate these heavenly treasures. Our focus should actually be on amassing these treasures. Just as we focus on our earthly net worth and the size of our checkbook or stock portfolios, we should even more pay attention to our heavenly net worth. The second point to consider is that we are instructed to lay up these treasures for ourselves. Christ is not telling us to accumulate treasures for others, but rather is appealing to our own self-interest by instructing us to focus on accumulating heavenly treasure for ourselves. We are to be motivated by a sense of self-interest.

Finally, Christ instructs us where to lay up our treasure—in heaven—as opposed to on earth. Our focus should be on accumulating assets in the eternal as opposed to the temporal.[2]

Another example of Christ's teaching on eternal rewards is contained in Matthew 13:44:

> "The kingdom of heaven is like treasure hidden in a field. When a man found it, he hid it again, and then in his joy went and sold all he had and bought that field."

In this parable, a man seemingly wandering through a field that was not his own finds a treasure that apparently has been hidden for a long time. Leaving the field, the man then hid the treasure again and with a sense of excitement and anticipation, sold everything he owned to purchase the field and possess the treasure he had found. The point is that the man's perspective and life changed once he found the treasure. You can imagine the man thinking about it, losing sleep at night pondering how wonderful it would be to own it, and obsessing about how his life would change once he possessed the treasure. He then gladly packed up everything in his house to take it to the pawnshop to sell it in order to accumulate enough money to purchase the plot of land where the treasure was located. The man did not hesitate and had no regrets—he realized that the treasure in the field had far more worth than the things he had already accumulated. Our attitude toward heaven should be the same—once we really realize how wonderful the treasure Christ has in store for us in heaven will be, we should be obsessed with it and gladly do everything we can—sell everything we have—to possess it. Why? Out of self-interest. Because the treasure in God's "field" is far more valuable and lasting than any earthly treasure we may have accumulated.

When I was in college, I was heavily involved in student government at a major university. I remember having debates with various people

---

[2] For further study of eternal rewards, I would highly recommend Randy Alcorn's book, *The Treasure Principle.*

about what an ideal society would be like. Being a Christian, I used to think that capitalism wasn't ideal because it led to selfishness and the accumulation of wealth. Surely, if Christ were to setup His earthly kingdom or create a utopian society, it would look more like socialism where everyone would play a role and share equally in the wealth that is generated. Having said that, I would argue with my fellow students that since mankind is sinful in nature and ultimately corrupt, capitalism was a more effective governing principle since it appealed to our innate sinful nature. True socialism on earth would only lead to corruption, which is why I believed and would argue for the former. I was essentially arguing that capitalism and motivation by self-interest was the lesser of two evils.

Having studied the nature of Christ's kingdom and the parables above, however, I'm now convinced that this isn't true. Although we shouldn't necessarily be motivated by accumulating money on earth, Jesus clearly instructs us to "store up *for [ourselves]* treasure in heaven". Jesus knows that we are motivated by self-interest and designed His Kingdom such that desiring *eternal rewards* isn't bad, but exactly what we should be doing! Selfishness occurs only when we pursue gain at the expense of others, but Christ's Kingdom isn't zero-sum—God has infinite treasure and will freely reward those that lived good lives and accomplished great things for the Kingdom. So, is it wrong to be motivated by reward? No. If it were, Christ wouldn't have offered it to us as a motivation.

Bruce Wilkenson in his book *A Life That God Rewards* makes the point that belief/grace unlocks the door to eternal life and determines *where* we will spend eternity, but our behavior unlocks the door to reward and determines *how* we will spend eternity. Our eternal destination is the consequence of what we believe on earth, but our eternal compensation is the consequence of how we behave on earth. These points are very true and the reason we should indeed be focused on accumulating God's eternal rewards.

When will we receive these rewards? Many think that we will receive them when we die and enter heaven, but this is not the case.

The Bible states that these rewards will be given out when Christ returns to the earth prior to setting up His Millennial kingdom on earth. Evidence of this is found in Matthew 16:27 which says "For the Son of Man will come in the glory of His Father with His angels, and then He will reward each according to his works" and in Revelation 22:12: "And behold, I am coming quickly, and My reward is with Me, to give to every one according to his work."

What will these rewards actually be? The Bible doesn't provide much detail, but we do know that position and authority are among the primary rewards. When Christ was on earth, He taught that each believer is "entrusted" with various talents and resources during their lifetimes. Our goal is to make the best use of these resources for furthering the kingdom. Believers who are faithful with the things God gave us while on earth will be entrusted with even more in Christ's kingdom, while those that were not will be entrusted with very little on Christ's kingdom (Matthew 25:14–30; Luke 19:12–26). We are also told that we will "judge angels" (1 Corinthians 6:3) and be "priests of God and of Christ and [we] will reign with Him" (Revelation 20:6), clearly showing that faithful Christians will have significant positions of authority in the afterlife. This only makes sense. The kingdom of Christ—the Millennial kingdom—will be a society very similar to what we live in today. It will include businesses, departments of government, courts, etc. When Christ returns, He will establish this kingdom and it's only logical that He would choose those who were most faithful and obedient to Him during their lives to serve as His appointments to these positions of leadership.

WHAT WILL REWARDS BE GIVEN FOR?

We have seen that Christ will provide rewards for those who faithfully served Him during their lifetimes and that we should eagerly seek to accumulate these rewards in heaven. We have also seen what these rewards will be—namely, positions of leadership and authority in His kingdom among other things. The question that begs asking then is what will these eternal rewards be given for? What specifically can we do while on earth to ensure we are "laying up" these rewards for ourselves in heaven?

The Bible states that eternal rewards are given for many different things. They are given:

- For seeking God (Hebrews 11:6) and for praying to Him (Matthew 6:6). God rewards those that eagerly seek to have a deeper relationship with Him.

- For sacrifices made in life to do Christian service (Matthew 16:24–27). This includes the denial of earthly pursuits and personal sacrifices made to further the kingdom. To those that have given up homes and family members to do Christian work (such as missionaries), Christ promises that the return will be a hundredfold (Matthew 19:29).

- For suffering and persecution. This includes physical suffering for Christ, as well as suffering in reputation, position, and stature (Luke 6:22–23; James 1:12; Revelation 2:10).

- For faithfully serving in roles of Church leadership (1 Peter 5:4).

- For giving money to the needy generously and anonymously (Matthew 6:3–4, 10:42, 19:21; 1 Timothy 6:18–19). The conditions on these verses make it clear that our motives, and not just the size of our giving, directly relates to our eternal reward. Matthew 6:1 states, "Take heed that you do not do your charitable deeds before men, to be seen by them. Otherwise you have no reward from your Father in heaven" and 1 Corinthians 13:3 says "though I bestow all my goods to feed the poor, and though I give my body to be burned, but have not love, it profits me nothing." The point is that our giving must not be out of pride, self-interest, or to improve one's reputation, but rather out of a genuine and compassionate heart.

- For showing compassion to the needy (Luke 14:13–14) and serving others in the name of Christ (Mark 9:41).

- For treating enemies kindly and doing good without expecting anything in return (Luke 6:35).

- For submitting to our employers and doing good in the positions we've been given (Ephesians 6:8; Colossians 3:22–24).

- For eagerly anticipating His Second Coming (2 Timothy 4:8). That's right—there is a special reward just for those that eagerly look forward to Christ's return!

- For helping lead others to faith in Christ (Philippians 4:1, 1 Thessalonians 2:19).

As can be seen, eternal rewards are given for many things. However, it's important to note that the rewards are not necessarily absolute, but rather relative in nature. This means that God not only will look at the deeds that we've done and the motives for those deeds, but He will also look for the value of those deeds relative to what we could have done. Christ taught this concept in two different parables. The first is the parable of the talents (Matthew 25:14–30) in which a man goes on a journey and entrusts his money to three different men. Each invested the money differently and received a different level of return.   The first two servants invested their money wisely and received a commendation, but the one who did not was chastised. One of the key points of this parable is that the servants' rewards were based on the total results they achieved in light of their potential, since each servant was given a different amount of money according to his own ability—yet received the same commendation and reward.   We can conclude from this that God's level of expectation for us—and the commensurate level of reward—is relative to the gifts, talents, and resources we've been given.

The second parable that teaches this concept is the parable of the minas (Luke 19). This parable is very similar to the parable of the talents, except that the master gave ten servants each an equivalent amount of money to invest. When the master returned from his trip, he inquired about what each servant had done with the money entrusted to him. The first servant achieved a tenfold return and was commended as a good and faithful servant. He was then given authority over ten cities. The second servant then came and reported a fivefold return. He was given a proportionate reward, but wasn't commended as good or faithful. The third servant who didn't do anything with the money that he was entrusted with was chastised. The implication from this parable is that the master knew that the second and third servants could have done more to multiply the money they had been given and yet did not.

These parables teach that our lives on earth are somewhat of a 'trial run' for eternity. God provides us each with different levels of resources and talents and He's looking to see how faithful we are with what He has entrusted to us. If we prove ourselves faithful while on earth, we will be rewarded accordingly in heaven. Yet if we fail to prove ourselves wise stewards while on earth, we won't necessarily receive a second chance while in heaven. In many ways, this is similar to the nature of our human institutions today. If a business associate, executive, teacher, or graduate student proves himself to be faithful and capable with small projects, they will subsequently be rewarded with larger projects. However, if we fail to show ourselves capable and trustworthy in small matters, we are seldom given a second chance or larger opportunities in the future.

WHAT WILL WE DO IN ETERNITY?

Many people think about eternity and react somewhat negatively. The images they have in their mind is of spending an endless existence strumming a harp on a cloud and wonder if anything could be more boring. It's not an exciting thought, is it? Given this mental image, many of us would prefer to just cease to exist. The alternative mental picture many of us have is to be in a celestial choir singing day in and day out. Although this image may be appealing to some, to many it may appear as equally unattractive.

Although there will certainly be worshiping in heaven (Revelation 19:5–6), is there anything more? What will we really be doing for eternity? Fortunately, the Bible does provide us with some clues. As we have already seen, Jesus will assign responsibilities in His kingdom commensurate with the faithfulness we displayed on earth (Revelation 22:3–4). These responsibilities will include authority over 'cities' and various positions of leadership. In the section on angels, we've seen that the spirit beings have an organization and structure similar to a modern government or similar organization. In describing Satan prior to his fall, the Bible states that he was known for his "widespread trade" (Ezekiel 28:16) and that "nations who knew you" were "appalled" (Ezekiel 28:19).

The implication of all these references is that heaven and eternity will be organized similarly to any system of government or modern city of today. There will be different roles and tasks necessary for the functioning of the city, and different people will have different levels of responsibility. Some may be involved in the arts, while others in sports, worship, commerce, etc. Likely, people will do many different things and try many different roles over time. The key point is that heaven and eternity will not be unlike living in a society on earth today, so whatever you enjoy doing today you will likely be able to continue into eternity. There are some obvious exceptions (i.e. doctors, nurses, police officers, fire fighters, and the like won't be needed), but for the most part, it is quite likely that the activities and responsibilities we will enjoy in heaven will be more similar to what we're currently familiar with on earth than the mental image of strumming a harp on a cloud that many of us have.

ETERNAL PERSPECTIVE

This article started with a simple instruction given to us in Colossians 3:2: "Set your minds on things above, not on earthly things."

The conclusion we should draw from this verse is that our energy, focus, and activities should be influenced by our contemplation and understanding of the spirit world. This is at the very core of our faith. As Christians, the perspective we have of our existence in the afterlife should impact the way we live our lives each day.

The Bible frequently uses terms such as "aliens", "strangers", "ambassadors" and the like to describe how Christians should view our role in this present world (Hebrews 11:13; 2 Corinthians 5:20). We're told that our citizenship is in heaven and that we belong to a "better country" (Philippians 3:20; Hebrews 11:16). The point is, we should not become too attached to this present world and instead should view everything we do from the perspective of our time being very limited on earth.

I'm getting there!

I travel quite a bit on business and recently have been spending some time in Italy. My citizenship is in the U.S., and my wife and two young boys live in Seattle. When I am planning my travels, I've noticed that the people in my group take two distinctly different approaches. Some will plan their travel so that they will be able to spend several extra days over the weekend in Italy so they can enjoy Italy's pleasures—including shopping, touring the historic sites, and visiting Italy's many fine restaurants. My approach, however, is very different. I plan my travels so that I can leave on a Sunday night, do business for my company from early morning to late evening, and fly out as soon as my business is done—frequently taking red-eye flights in both directions. Although I appreciate all that Italy has to offer, my heart is in the U.S. where I desire to spend as much time as possible with my family. I want to be productive on my trips and focus on completing my company's business rather than satisfying my own pleasures.

Although your perspective on business travel may be different than mine, the analogy to heaven is similar. Our citizenship is in heaven and our time on earth should be viewed as an extended business trip. While we are here, we can spend our time enjoying the pleasures that the earth has to offer and this isn't always bad, but what we need to realize is that we will be rewarded in heaven for how productively we spent our time and what eternal results we achieved. God wants us to be faithful servants who He can entrust with talents and resources, knowing that we will apply them to good use during the short time we have on earth.

The famous theologian John Wesley once said "I judge all things only by the price they shall gain in eternity." How wonderful it would be if we could all have such a clear perspective of the value of eternal rewards, and of the mission we should have while on earth. Likewise, the missionary Jim Elliot wrote "He is no fool who gives what he cannot keep to gain what he cannot lose." Jim Elliot, who was killed in Ecuador trying to reach remote tribes with the gospel message, clearly understood that everything we have on earth is worthless compared to the eternal value of what God has for us in heaven. In comparison to the length of our lives in eternity—which we can't even begin to comprehend—our lives on earth represent nothing more than a very small speck of time. In light of this, where would you rather invest your time and energy?

Paul demonstrated a keen understanding and perspective of this tradeoff as well. While in prison awaiting either a death sentence or an acquittal, Paul debated:

> "For to me, to live is Christ and to die is gain. If I am to go on living in the body, this will mean fruitful labor for me. Yet what shall I choose? I do not know! I am torn between the two: I desire to depart and be with Christ, which is better by far; but it is

more necessary for you that I remain in the body." (Philippians 1:21–23).

Paul actually could not decide whether it was better to die and be in heaven with Christ, or whether it was better to remain on earth and continue his work for the kingdom! Paul clearly grasped the nature of the afterlife and the importance of his daily mission on earth.

Hebrews 11 in the Bible is known as the 'faith chapter' because it outlines 'heroes of the faith'—people who were especially faithful during their lifetimes and in their service to God. People included in this biblical hall of fame include Abel, Enoch, Noah, Abraham, Isaac, Jacob, Joseph, Moses, Rahab, and several others. What's interesting is the nature of the commendation that God gives them:

> "All these people were still living by faith when they died. They did not receive the things promised; they only saw them and welcomed them from a distance. And they admitted that they were aliens and strangers on earth. People who say such things show that they are looking for a country of their own. If they had been thinking of the country they had left, they would have had opportunity to return. Instead, they were longing for a better country – a heavenly one. Therefore God is not ashamed to be called their God, for he has prepared a city for them." (Hebrews 11:12–16).

God called these people out because of their faith—not in earthly things, but in heavenly things. Each of these people knew their citizenship was in heaven and what God had in store for them was infinitely more important and valuable than the homes, families, and careers that they may have left. Each was longing for their real home—and each was commended by God and promised an eternal reward ("a city") in return. If this is the type of people that the Bible calls out, and living for the eternal is what they are commended for, should our perspective, attitude, and lives not be similar?

When my grandmother was on her deathbed dying from cancer, I had the opportunity to sit beside her a few days before she passed away.

She asked me to read her Revelation 21, which I did. Revelation 21 is the chapter of the Bible that describes the new heaven and the new earth. Why would she ask me to read this passage so close to the end of her life? Because she understood our hope as believers. She understood that her life was not ending, but rather she was about to return to the country to which she really belonged. She was about to conclude her business on earth and be welcomed by Christ into His kingdom to spend eternity in the wonderfulness of God and heaven. We are instructed to set our minds on things above, and her pending death had clearly focused her mind on the promises, rewards, and blessings that await us in the next world.

Someone once said, "It ought to be the business of every day to prepare for our last day." I hope that, through a better understanding of the afterlife and the nature of God's kingdom, we will all be better at living with an eternal perspective.

Made in the USA
San Bernardino, CA
05 January 2014